Design: Judith Chant and Alison Lee
Recipe Photography: Peter Barry
Jacket and Illustration Artwork: Jane Winton, courtesy of
Bernard Thornton Artists, London
Editor: Josephine Bacon

CLB 4262
This edition published in 1995 by
Whitecap Books Ltd., 351 Lynn Avenue,
North Vancouver, B.C., Canada V7J 2C4

Printed in Singapore
ISBN 1-55110-218-8

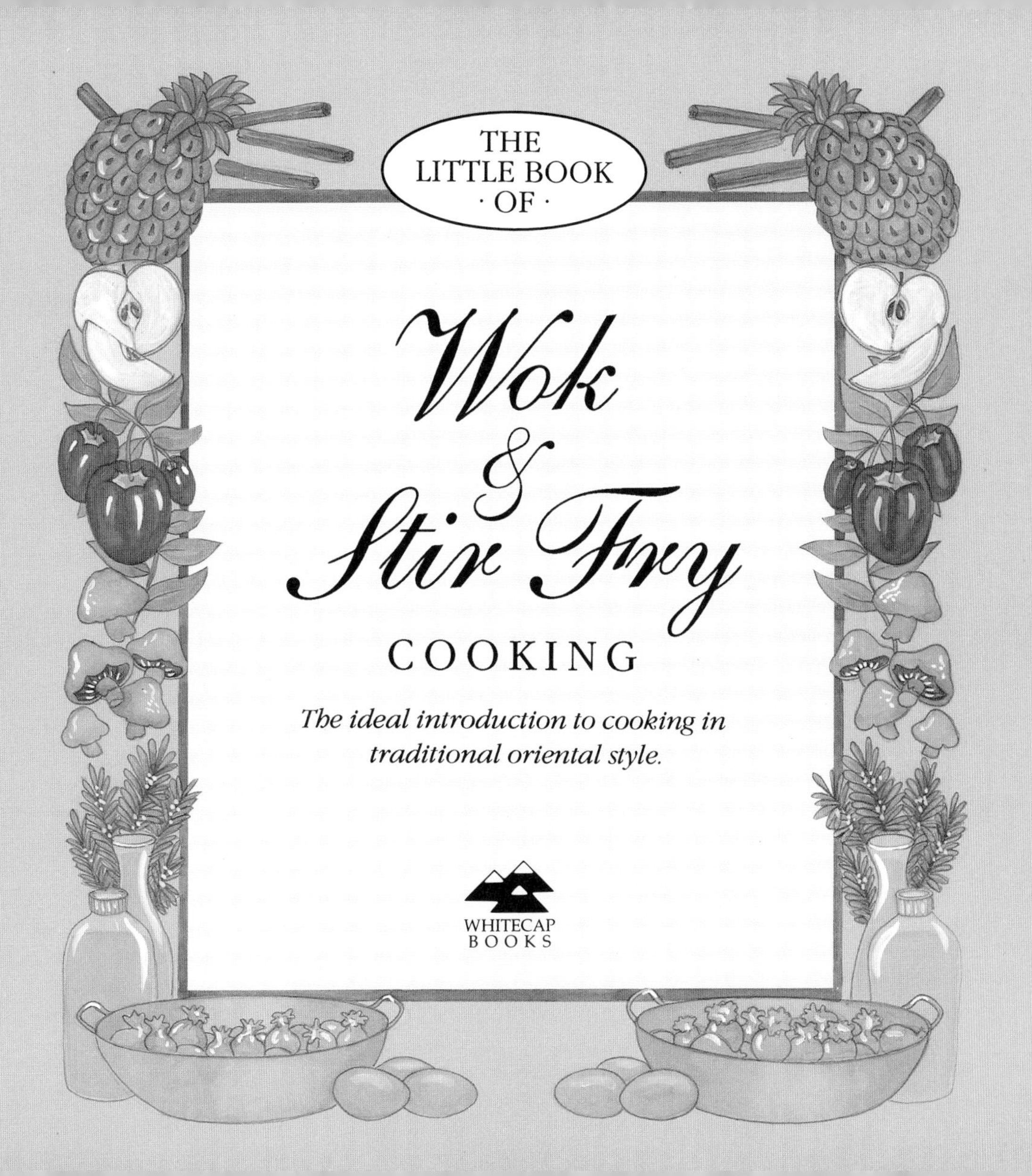

THE LITTLE BOOK · OF ·

Wok & Stir Fry COOKING

The ideal introduction to cooking in traditional oriental style.

WHITECAP BOOKS

Introduction

The widespread popularity of Oriental cuisine has led to a great surge in the use of the wok. A wok is a deep skillet with rounded sides and a domed lid. It originates from China and is seen all over the Far East, where foods are often prepared, cooked and sold on busy street-corners. This Oriental pan is a wonderfully versatile piece of equipment, as it can be used not only for stir-frying, but is also very effective for deep-frying and, when fitted with a wooden trivet, for steaming. Woks have become a hot item to such an extent that they are now widely available in kitchen equipment stores, and not just in a few Chinatown grocery stores, as was the case only a few years ago.

Traditionally shaped woks are designed to be used on gas stoves. The rounded nature of the pan allows the gas flame to heat the sides, so giving a wider heat distribution and cooking the food more evenly, rather than just cooking the food on the bottom of pan. Western manufacturers, however, have produced flat-bottomed woks designed especially for electric stoves. These distribute the heat around the wok in a similar way to conventional woks. When buying a wok for the first time, it is essential to buy the right type for your stove.

Stir-frying is the extremely quick and wonderfully easy method of cooking most closely associated with the wok. A small amount of oil is heated in the wok, and the freshly prepared ingredients, which are usually cut small enough to cook quickly, are stir-fried for only a few minutes until everything is just cooked through. Stir-fried foods should never be soggy and overcooked. Vegetables, in particular, should still have a crunch to them, and meats should be seared on the outside and soft and melting on the inside. Speed is the essence of stir-fry cooking, and the food should be equally speedily served, and never kept hanging around. The best oil to use for stir-frying is a vegetable oil such as sunflower or peanut oil (also known as groundnut oil), and always remember to heat the wok thoroughly before the oil is added. Olive oil, butter or margarine are not suitable for stir-frying as these fats are for use at lower temperatures only and will burn if subjected to the intense heat of a wok.

The step-by-step instructions in this book explain how to stir-fry delicious Chinese-style dishes of lightly spiced meats, fish, and vegetables – and even fruit desserts – in the minimum time with the minimum effort.

Sesame Chicken Wings

SERVES 8

This inexpensive dish makes a great cocktail snack or appetizer, or serve as a light meal with stir-fried vegetables.

PREPARATION: 25 mins
COOKING: 14 mins

---

12 chicken wings
1 tbsp salted black beans
1 tbsp water
1 tbsp oil
2 cloves garlic, crushed
2 slices fresh ginger, cut into fine shreds
3 tbsps soy sauce
1½ tbsps dry sherry or rice wine
Large pinch of black pepper
1 tbsp sesame seeds
Green onions (scallions) or coriander (cilantro) leaves to garnish

---

1. Cut off and discard the chicken wing tips. Cut between the joint to separate the wings into two pieces.

2. Crush the beans and add the water. Leave to stand.

3. Heat the oil in a wok and add the garlic and ginger. Stir briefly and add the chicken wings.

Step 1 Using a knife or scissors, cut through the joint in the wings and separate them into two pieces.

Cook, stirring, until lightly browned – about 3 minutes. Add the soy sauce and wine and cook, stirring, about 30 seconds longer. Add the soaked black beans and pepper.

4. Cover the wok tightly and allow to simmer about 8-10 minutes. Uncover and turn the heat to high. Continue cooking, stirring until the liquid is almost evaporated and the chicken wings are glazed with sauce.

5. Remove from the heat and sprinkle with the sesame seeds. Stir to coat completely and serve. Garnish with green onions (scallions) or coriander (cilantro).

Pork Spareribs with Chinese Mushrooms

SERVES 4

Spareribs served with Chinese mushrooms (cloud ears) in a slightly hot and spicy sauce make a delicious appetizer or entrée.

PREPARATION: 15 mins
COOKING: 20 mins

---

2 pounds pork spareribs
1 carrot, finely sliced
1 leek, finely chopped
1 bayleaf
⅔ cup dried Chinese mushrooms (cloud ears), soaked 15 minutes in warm water and drained
1 tbsp oil
1 tsp chopped garlic
½ tsp chili sauce
1 tbsp soy sauce
1 tbsp hoisin sauce
1 tsp wine vinegar
1¼ cups chicken broth
Salt and pepper

---

1. Cut the spareribs down the bone to separate them. Then cut them into smaller pieces, so that they are easier to handle. In a medium-sized, flameproof casserole bring to the boil plenty of water along with the carrot, leek, and bayleaf. Blanch the spareribs for 1 minute in the boiling water. Remove and drain well.

Step 1 Blanch the spareribs in boiling water 1 minute.

Step 1 Remove the blanched ribs and drain well.

2. Cook the mushrooms in the boiling water for 10 minutes. Drain well, discarding the water.

3. Heat the oil in a wok, add the garlic, chili sauce, and the mushrooms. Fry slowly until lightly colored.

4. Stir in the soy sauce, hoisin sauce, vinegar, and broth.

5. Add the spareribs, stirring all the ingredients together well. Season with salt and pepper to taste and cook, covered, for 10 minutes.

6. Remove the lid and allow the sauce to reduce slightly. Serve piping hot.

Gado Gado

SERVES 4

This makes a very appealing appetizer for a dinner party based on Chinese or Indonesian dishes.

PREPARATION: 20 mins
COOKING: 30 mins

1 tbsp peanut oil
1 carrot, cut into thin strips
1 potato, cut into thin strips
½ cup green beans, trimmed
½ cup Chinese (Nappa) cabbage, shredded
½ cup beansprouts
½ a cucumber, cut into batons

Peanut Sauce
2 tbsps peanut oil
½ cup raw shelled peanuts
2 red chilies, seeded and finely chopped, or 1 tsp chili powder
2 shallots, finely chopped
1 clove garlic, crushed
⅔ cup water
1 tsp brown sugar
Juice of ½ lemon
Salt
⅓ cup unsweetened coconut milk
Sliced hard-cooked eggs, to garnish
Sliced cucumber, to garnish

1. Heat a wok and add 1 tbsp peanut oil. When hot, add the carrot and potato. Stir-fry 2 minutes and add green beans and cabbage. Cook a further 3 minutes.
2. Add the beansprouts and cucumber, and stir-fry 2 minutes. Place on a serving platter and keep warm.
3. To make the peanut sauce, heat the wok, add 2 tbsps peanut oil, and fry the peanuts for 2-3 minutes. Remove and drain on kitchen paper.
4. Blend or pound the chilies, shallots, and garlic to a smooth paste. Grind or blend peanuts to a powder.
5. Reheat the oil and fry the chili paste 2 minutes.
6. Add the water, and bring to the boil. Add peanuts, brown sugar, lemon juice, and salt to taste. Stir about 10 minutes or until the sauce is thick, and add coconut milk.
7. Garnish the vegetables with slices of hard-cooked egg and cucumber, and serve with the peanut sauce.

P
S

Beef with Onions

SERVES 4

Serve this marinated beef dish with plain rice or noodles.

PREPARATION: 15 mins plus 30 minutes marinating
COOKING: 20 mins

1 pound fillet steak
1 tbsp oil
1 piece fresh ginger root, peeled and roughly chopped
3 onions, finely sliced
1 clove garlic, chopped
1¼ cups beef broth
Pinch of sugar
2 tbsps dark soy sauce
1 tsp cornstarch, combined with a little water
Salt and pepper

Marinade
1 tbsp oil
1 tsp sesame oil
1 tbsp rice wine

1. Cut the fillet into very thin slices across the grain.

2. Mix together the marinade ingredients and stir in the meat. Leave to marinate for 30 minutes.

3. Heat the oil in a wok and sauté the ginger, onions, and garlic until lightly browned.

4. Remove the meat from the marinade with a slotted spoon and discard the marinade. Add the meat to the wok and stir-fry with the vegetables.

Step 5 Add the broth, sugar, and soy sauce. Cook for 4 minutes.

5. Pour over the stock, sugar, and soy sauce. Cook for 4 minutes.

6. Add the cornstarch mixture to the sauce, stirring continuously until thickened. Season with salt and pepper and serve immediately.

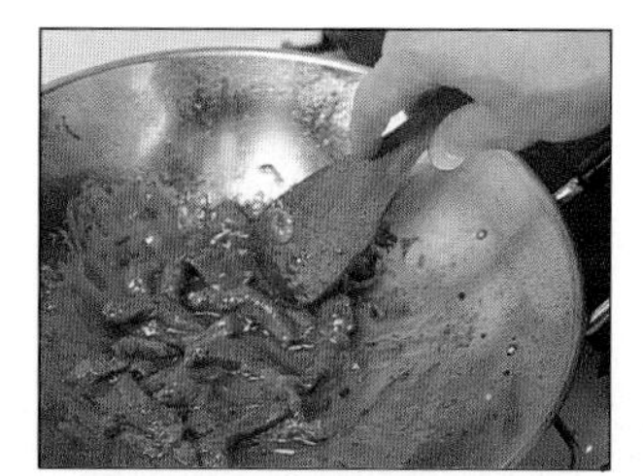

Step 6 Add the cornstarch mixture to the wok and stir continuously until thickened.

Deep-Fried Chicken with Lemon Slices

SERVES 6

This delicious dish seems to have lots of ingredients, but it is really quite simple to make.

PREPARATION: 30 mins
COOKING: 15 mins

3 pounds boneless chicken breast
6 tbsps cornstarch
3 tbsps all-purpose flour
1 green bell pepper
1 red bell pepper
Oil for deep-frying

Marinade
½ tsp salt
½ tbsp red wine
½ tbsp light soy sauce
1 tbsp cornstarch
1 tbsp water
1 egg yolk
Black pepper

Sauce
3 tbsps sugar
3 tbsps lemon juice
6 tbsps chicken broth
½ tsp salt
2 tbsps cornstarch
1 tsp sesame oil

2 lemons to garnish, thinly sliced
Chopped parsley to garnish

1. Skin the chicken. Cut into thin bite-sized slices.

2. Mix all the marinade ingredients together and marinate the chicken in the mixture for 10 minutes.

3. Mix the cornstarch and all-purpose flour together on a plate, remove the chicken from the marinade, and coat each chicken piece with the flour mixture.

4. Mix all the sauce ingredients together in a small bowl. Cut the peppers into 1-inch pieces.

5. Place a wok over a high heat. Heat the oil until almost smoking. Deep-fry the chicken slices until golden-brown. Remove with a slotted spoon to a heated plate. Pour off all but 1 tbsp of the oil.

6. Stir-fry the peppers until they begin to brown. Add the sauce and bring to the boil, stirring until thickened. Add the chicken pieces. Stir for a few more minutes.

7. Transfer to a heated serving platter, and garnish with lemon slices and chopped parsley.

Duck with Bamboo Shoots

SERVES 4

Stir-fried bamboo shoots, served with duck breasts and a hoisin-based sauce.

PREPARATION: 10 mins
COOKING: 50 mins

1 cup canned bamboo shoots, cut into thin slices
3 tbsps sugar
⅔ cup water
1 tsp chopped fresh ginger root
1 tbsp hoisin sauce
2 uncooked duck breasts
1 tbsp oil
Salt and pepper

1. Cook the bamboo shoots in boiling, lightly salted water for about 15 minutes. Drain thoroughly and set aside.

2. Mix the sugar and water together in a small saucepan, stirring thoroughly.

Step 3 Add the hoisin sauce to the pan. Place over a gentle heat and cook until a light syrup is formed.

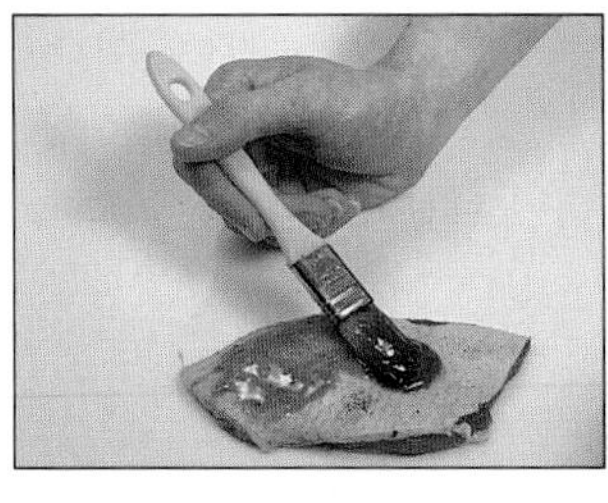

Step 4 Brush the syrup liberally over the duck breasts.

3. Add the ginger and the hoisin sauce. Place over a gentle heat and cook until a light syrup is formed.

4. Brush this syrup liberally over the duck breasts.

5. Heat the oil in a skillet or wok and add the duck breasts, skin-side down first. Sear on each side. Take out and finish cooking in an oven preheated to 425°F, for about 15 minutes.

6. When the duck breasts have been in the oven 5 minutes, stir-fry the bamboo shoots in the oil used to sear the duck breasts. Season with salt and pepper and serve hot with the sliced duck breasts. Serve any leftover sauce in a small bowl to accompany the duck.

Stir-Fried Leeks and Lamb

SERVES 4

Rosemary, jelly and mint are all classic accompaniments to lamb and complement it perfectly.

PREPARATION: 10 mins
COOKING: 30 mins

1 tbsp oil
2 tsps fresh rosemary
2 tsps fresh basil leaves, chopped
2 cups leeks, cut into 1-inch slices
1 pound lean, boneless lamb, cut into 1-inch cubes
14-ounce can plum tomatoes
1 tsp cranberry jelly
1 tbsp chopped fresh mint
Salt and pepper
Fresh mint to garnish

1. Heat a wok and add the oil. Add the rosemary, basil, and leeks, and stir-fry gently 3 minutes. Remove from the wok, and increase the heat.

2. Add the lamb and stir-fry until well-browned all over.

3. Return the leeks to the wok. Add the undrained tomatoes, cranberry jelly, mint, and salt and pepper to taste.

4. Cover and simmer 20 minutes, adding water if necessary. Serve hot, garnished with fresh mint.

Shrimp and Scallop Stir-Fry

SERVES 4

Pine nuts and spinach give originality to this delicious dish.

PREPARATION: 35 mins
COOKING: 10 mins

3 tbsps oil
4 tbsps pine nuts
1 pound raw shrimp, peeled
1 pound scallops, quartered if large
2 tsps grated fresh root ginger
1 small red or green chili, seeded and finely chopped
2 cloves garlic, finely chopped
1 large red bell pepper, cut into 1-inch diagonal pieces
3 cups fresh spinach, stalks removed, leaves well-washed and shredded
4 green onions (scallions), cut in ½-inch diagonal pieces
4 tbsps fish or chicken broth
4 tbsps light soy sauce
4 tbsps rice wine or dry sherry
1 tbsp cornstarch

1. Heat the oil in a wok and add the pine nuts. Cook over low heat, stirring continuously until lightly browned. Remove with a skimmer and drain on kitchen paper.

2. Add the shrimp and scallops to the oil remaining in the wok and stir over a moderate heat until the scallops are beginning to look white and firm, and the shrimp look pink.

Step 1 Cook the pine nuts in the oil until lightly browned.

3. Add the ginger, chili, garlic, and red bell pepper and cook a few minutes over a moderate heat.

4. Add the spinach and green onions (scallions), and stir-fry briefly. Mix the remaining ingredients together and pour over the contents of the wok.

5. Increase the heat to bring the liquid to the boil, stirring ingredients constantly. Once the liquid thickens and clears, stir in the pine nuts and serve immediately.

Step 5 Add the liquid to the pan and cook until it thickens to a sauce.

Spiced Beef

SERVES 4

This robust stir-fry dish is good served with steamed Chinese greens.

PREPARATION: 30 mins
COOKING: 5-6 mins

Marinade
1 tsp sugar
2-3 star anise, ground
½ tsp ground fennel seeds
1 tbsp dark soy sauce
¼ tsp monosodium glutamate (optional)

1 pound fillet of beef, cut into 1-inch strips
1-inch piece fresh root ginger, peeled and crushed
½ tsp salt
2 tbsps oil
4 green onions (scallions), sliced
½ tsp freshly ground black pepper
1 tbsp light soy sauce

1. Mix the marinade ingredients together in a bowl.

2. Add the beef strips, ginger and salt. Stir well together to coat and marinate 20 minutes.

3. Heat the oil in a wok. Add the green onions (scallions) and stir-fry for 1 minute.

4. Add the beef, ground pepper, and the light soy sauce and stir-fry 4-5 minutes. Serve with a dip.

Cantonese Egg Fu Yong

SERVES 2-3

As the name suggests, this dish is from Canton. However, fu yong dishes are popular in other parts of China.

PREPARATION: 25 mins
COOKING: 12 mins

5 eggs
¼ cup shredded cooked meat, poultry, or fish
1 celery stick, finely shredded
4 dried Chinese mushrooms, soaked in boiling water for 5 minutes
¼ cup bean sprouts
1 small onion, thinly sliced
Pinch of salt and pepper
1 tsp dry sherry
Oil for frying

Sauce
1 tbsp cornstarch dissolved in 3 tbsps cold water
1¼ cups chicken broth
1 tsp tomato ketchup
1 tbsp soy sauce
Pinch of salt and pepper
Dash of sesame oil

1. Beat the eggs lightly and add the shredded meat or fish and celery.

2. Squeeze all the liquid from the dried mushrooms. Discard the stems and cut the caps into thin slices. Add to the egg mixture along with the bean sprouts and onion. Add the seasoning and sherry, and stir well.

Step 3 Heat the oil in a wok and spoon in 3 fl oz of the egg mixture.

3. Heat a wok and pour in about 4 tbsps oil. When hot, carefully spoon in about 6 tbsps of the egg mixture.

4. Brown on one side, turn over gently and brown the other side. Remove the cooked omelet to a plate and continue until all the mixture has been used.

5. Combine all the sauce ingredients in a small, heavy-based pan and bring slowly to the boil, stirring continuously until thickened and cleared. Pour the sauce over the Egg Fu Yong to serve.

Chicken in Hot Pepper Sauce

SERVES 4

Stir-fried chicken served with peppers in a hot pepper sauce.

PREPARATION: 10 mins
COOKING: 25 mins

1½ pounds boneless chicken
2 tbsps oil
1 tsp chopped garlic
1 red bell pepper, cut into thin strips
1 green bell pepper, cut into thin strips
1 tsp white wine vinegar
1 tbsp light soy sauce
1 tsp sugar
1¼ cups chicken broth
1 tbsp chili sauce
Salt and pepper

1. Cut the chicken meat into thin strips. Heat the oil in a wok and stir-fry the garlic, chicken, and the green and red bell peppers.

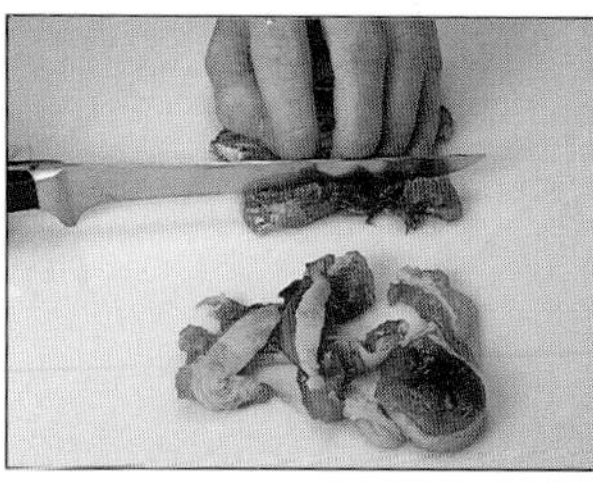

Step 1 Cut the chicken meat into thin strips.

2. Pour off any excess oil and deglaze the wok with the vinegar. Stir in the soy sauce, sugar, and broth.

3. Gradually stir in the chili sauce, tasting after each addition. Season with a little salt and pepper to taste.

4. Cook until the sauce has reduced slightly. Serve piping hot.

Beef with Tomato & Pepper in Black Bean Sauce

SERVES 4-6

Black beans are a specialty of Cantonese cooking and give a pungent, salty taste to stir-fried dishes.

PREPARATION: 25 mins
COOKING: 5 mins

2 large tomatoes
2 tbsps salted black beans
2 tbsps water
4 tbsps dark soy sauce
1 tbsp cornstarch
1 tbsp dry sherry
1 tsp sugar
1 pound rump steak, cut into thin strips
1 small green bell pepper
4 tbsps oil
⅔ cup beef broth
Pinch of ground black pepper

1. Core the tomatoes and cut them into

Step 1 Remove the cores from the tomatoes with a sharp knife. Cut into even-sized wedges.

Step 4 Add the beef mixture to the wok and stir-fry until the sauce thickens to glaze the meat.

wedges. Crush the black beans, add the water and set aside.

2. Combine the soy sauce, cornstarch, sherry, sugar, and meat in a bowl, and set aside.

3. Cut the pepper into ½-inch diagonal pieces. Heat a wok and add the oil. When hot, stir-fry the green bell pepper pieces about 1 minute and remove from the wok.

4. Add the meat and the soy sauce mixture to the wok and stir-fry about 2 minutes. Add the soaked black beans and the broth. Bring to the boil and allow to thicken slightly.

5. Return the pepper to the wok, and add the tomatoes and black pepper. Heat through 1 minute and serve immediately.

Sweet-and-Sour Pork with Pineapple

SERVES 4

This classic Chinese recipe is easy to prepare at home.

PREPARATION: 15 mins
COOKING: 20 mins

1 pound lean pork fillet, cut into 1-inch cubes
2 tbsps light soy sauce
2 tbsps white wine vinegar
2 tbsps tomato paste
1 tbsp sugar
2 tbsps peanut oil
1 tbsp cornstarch
1 clove garlic, crushed
1 tsp grated fresh root ginger
⅔ cup water
1 can pineapple pieces, drained
Fresh coriander (cilantro) to garnish

1. Place the pork in a bowl, pour the soy sauce over it, and toss together. Leave to marinate for 15 minutes.

2. Meanwhile, make the sauce by mixing together the vinegar, tomato paste, and sugar, and set aside.

3. Heat a wok and add the oil.

4. Remove the pork from soy sauce, and add the soy to the sauce mixture. Toss the pork in the cornstarch, coating well.

5. When the oil is hot, brown the pork well all over. Remove from the pan and reduce the heat.

6. Fry the garlic and ginger 30 seconds. Add the water. Bring to the boil, then return the pork to the wok.

7. Reduce the heat; cover, and simmer 15 minutes, stirring occasionally.

8. Add the sauce mixture and pineapple, and simmer for a further 15 minutes. Garnish with coriander (cilantro) leaves.

Stir-Fried Rice with Peppers

SERVES 3-4

Red and green bell peppers, onions, and soy sauce add color as well as flavor to this rice dish.

PREPARATION: 5 mins
COOKING: 25 mins

½ cup long-grain rice
1 tbsp peanut oil
1 onion, chopped
1 green bell pepper, cut into small pieces
1 red bell pepper, cut into small pieces
1 tbsp soy sauce
Salt and pepper
1 tsp sesame oil

Step 2 Heat the oil in a wok and stir-fry the onion and peppers until lightly browned.

Step 3 Add the cooked rice to the wok and stir in the soy sauce.

1. Cook the rice in 1½ cups boiling water until just tender. Drain and set aside.

2. Heat the oil in a wok and stir-fry the onion. Add the peppers and fry until lightly browned.

3. Add the rice to the wok, stir in the soy sauce and continue cooking until the rice is heated through completely.

4. Season with salt, pepper, and the sesame oil, and serve.

Stir-Fried Sticky Rice

SERVES 4

Glutinous (sticky) rice cooked with stir-fried mushrooms, ginger, and shallots makes a delicious accompaniment to an entrée.

PREPARATION: 5 mins
COOKING: 25 mins

1 cup uncooked glutinous (sticky) rice
2 tbsps oil
2 green onions (scallions), chopped
½ onion, chopped
1 slice fresh ginger root
4 dried Chinese black mushrooms, soaked for 15 minutes in warm water, drained, and sliced
Salt and pepper

1. Wash the rice in plenty of cold water and place it in a sieve. Pour 5 ⅔ cups boiling water over the rice.

Step 4 Add the rice to the wok and stir in well.

Step 4 Pour in enough water to cover the rice by ½ inch.

2. Heat the oil in a wok and stir-fry the green onions (scallions), onion, and ginger until golden-brown.

3. Add the mushrooms and continue cooking, stirring and shaking the wok frequently.

4. Drain the rice and add to the wok, stirring well. Pour enough water over the rice to cover it by ½ inch.

5. Cover and cook over a moderate heat until there is almost no liquid left. Reduce the heat once again and continue cooking until all the liquid has been absorbed. This takes about 20 minutes in total.

6. Add salt and pepper to taste and serve immediately.

Peking Taffy Apples

SERVES 4

A quick and easy dessert to prepare and one which you never grow out of!

PREPARATION: 10 mins
COOKING: 30 mins

4 crisp apples
1 egg
¼ cup all-purpose flour
Oil for deep-frying
6 tbsps sugar
3 tbsps oil
3 tbsps dark corn syrup

1. Peel, core, and thickly slice the apples.

2. Blend the egg, flour, and 4 tbsps water to make a smooth mixture.

3. Place oil for deep-frying in a wok and heat to a moderate temperature, about 350°F.

4. Dip the apple slices in the mixture just before frying. Deep-fry several slices at a time, for 2-3 minutes or until golden. Drain on kitchen paper, and keep warm.

5. Heat the sugar, oil, and 2 tbsps water in a pan over a low heat, until the sugar dissolves. Turn up the heat and cook for about 5 minutes until the sugar starts to caramelize. Stir in the syrup and heat for a further 2 minutes.

6. Add the fried apple and stir slowly, covering each piece with syrup.

7. Quickly spoon hot, syrup-covered apples into a large bowl of iced water to harden syrup. Remove quickly and serve.

Step 6 Add the fritters to the syrup.

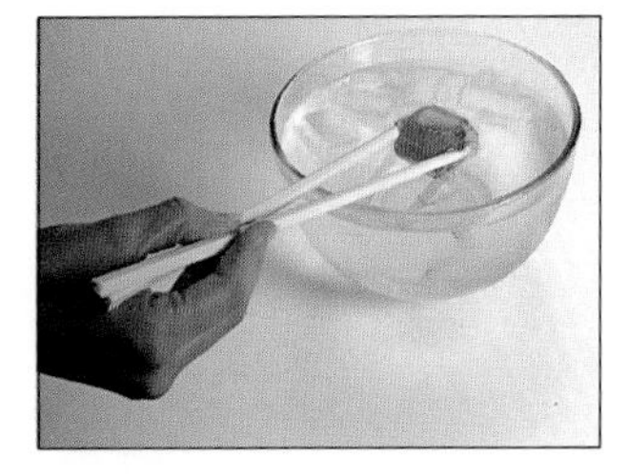

Step 7 Quickly spoon the syrup-covered apples into a large bowl of ice-water to harden the syrup. Remove quickly and serve.

Stir-Fried Fruit Salad

SERVES 4

In this unusual fruit salad, the exotic ingredients are stir-fried in a little oil, and delicately flavored with cinnamon.

PREPARATION: 30 mins
COOKING: 10 mins

4 slices fresh pineapple
1 grapefruit
2 pears
1 papaya
1 mango
12 lychees, peeled
2 tbsps oil
2 tbsps sugar
Ground cinnamon

1. Trim away the pineapple skin and cut the flesh into thin slices. Peel the grapefruit and cut it into segments. Peel the pears, the papaya, and mango, and cut the flesh into thin slices.

Step 1 Cut the pineapple into slices. Peel and segment the grapefruit. Peel and slice the pears, papaya, and mango.

2. Heat the oil and stir-fry the fruit in the following order: pineapple, lychees, mango, papaya, pears, and lastly the grapefruit.

3. Sprinkle with the sugar. Cook for a few more minutes and sprinkle with the cinnamon. Serve either hot or cold.

Sweet Bean Wontons

SERVES 6

Wonton snacks, either sweet or savory, are a popular teahouse treat in China. Made from prepared wonton wrappers and ready-made bean paste, these couldn't be simpler to make.

PREPARATION: 20 mins
COOKING: 20 mins

15 wonton wrappers
1 cup sweet red bean paste
1 tbsp cornstarch
¼ cup cold water
Oil for deep-frying
Honey

1. Take a wonton wrapper in the palm of your hand and place a little of the red bean paste slightly above the center.

Step 4 Pull the sides together and stick together with the cornstarch-and-water paste.

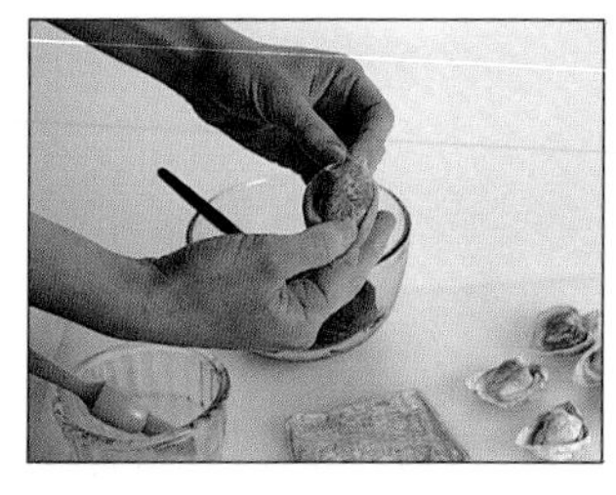

Step 5 Turn the wonton packages inside out by pushing the filled portion through the middle.

2. Mix together the cornstarch and water and moisten the edge around the filling.

3. Fold over diagonally, slightly off-center.

4. Pull the sides together, using the cornstarch-and-water paste to stick the two together.

5. Turn inside out by gently pushing the filled center through the middle.

6. Heat enough oil in a wok for deep frying and when hot, put in 4 of the filled wontons at a time. Cook until crisp and golden and remove to kitchen paper to drain. Repeat with the remaining filled wontons. Serve sprinkled with honey.

Index